MAGNETIC EQUATOR

MAGNETIC EQUATOR

KAIE KELLOUGH

McClelland & Stewart

McClelland & Stewart and colophon are registered trademarks
of Penguin Random House Canada Limited.

Published simultaneously in the United States of America by
McClelland & Stewart, a division of Penguin Random House Canada Limited.

Library and Archives Canada Cataloguing in Publication

Kellough, Kaie, 1975-, author
Magnetic equator / Kaie Kellough.

Issued in print and electronic formats.
ISBN 978-0-7710-4311-6 (softcover).—ISBN 978-0-7710-4312-3 (EPUB)

I. Title.

PS8571.E58643M34 2019   C811'.6   C2018-903251-0
                                                 C2018-903252-9

Typeset in Adobe Jenson by M&S, Toronto
Printed in the United States of America

McClelland & Stewart,
a division of Penguin Random House Canada Limited,
a Penguin Random House Company

www.penguinrandomhouse.ca

Penguin
Random House
McCLELLAND & STEWART

surely in that "smoke that thundered" there was a door

why make the smoke a door?

CONTENTS

kaieteur falls

potarorapidsfume}slide{e////////x}i{ûûûûûûûûûû}l{e|||||||||||||s}cascade{intothegreen

smokefallsupward}riddim{e|||||||||||||v}a{ûûûûûûûûûû}p{o\\\\\\\\r}sense{kiskadeesmist

yellowblur}ravings{a\\\\\\\\t}e{ûûûûûûûûûû}i{n////////t}bromeliads{rivershimmer

junglefrondsfurl}green{h|||||||||||||e}m{ûûûûûûûûûû}i{s|||||||||||||t}fronds{dreamsdangle

goldenfrogsstare}tropes{w////////a}f{ûûûûûûûûûû}t{i\\\\\\\\n}dread{pooleddewripples

waterthunders}unfurl{g|||||||||||||o}v{ûûûûûûûûûû}e{r////////t}voices{birdsflit&zip

lizardsfreeze}babble{h\\\\\\\\e}w{ûûûûûûûûûû}a{t|||||||||||||e}gibber{foamcascades

cacophonous}riddim{r|||||||||||||f}a{ûûûûûûûûûû}l{l\\\\\\\\g}bubbles{spiritlevel

greensphere}ravings{e////////n}e{ûûûûûûûûûû}r{a////////t}rise{arrowheadidea

timeless.creator}green{o|||||||||||||r}o{ûûûûûûûûûû}f{e|||||||||||||l}senses{earth'srockjaw

grinswidegapes}tumble{e\\\\\\\\c}t{ûûûûûûûûûû}r{i\\\\\\\\c}exiled{afarfrothingroar

envelopsvegetable}tropes{b|||||||||||||l}o{ûûûûûûûûûû}o{m////////s}froth{kingdomsound

rumblesechoes}blue{c////////r}e{ûûûûûûûûûû}o{l|||||||||||||e}distances{growth'sbustle

densitiesofpetals}solar{d|||||||||||||i}a{ûûûûûûûûûû}l{e\\\\\\\\c}gong{explodeexceed

ferntracefossil}resounds{t////////l}i{ûûûûûûûûûû}l{i|||||||||||||e}golden{leavesdecompose

dampmapforest}flower{s|||||||||||||h}o{ûûûûûûûûûû}o{t\\\\\\\\s}adrift{floorbreathingover

loverdevourer}mist{r\\\\\\\\u}s{ûûûûûûûûûû}t{e////////d}hoarse{earthomnivore

recyclescultures}roar{t|||||||||||||r}u{ûûûûûûûûûû}n{k|||||||||||||s}thrum{digestscenturies

issueslivingshoots}tropes{e////////s}c{ûûûûûûûûûû}a{p\\\\\\\\e}dread{plantrumination

orchid.heliconia}drone{m|||||||||||||a}p{ûûûûûûûûûû}m{a////////p}voice{victoriaamazonica

floweringfutures}soaked{c\\\\\\\\r}e{ûûûûûûûûûû}a{t|||||||||||||e}solar{sepalpetalpistil

stamentongue}riddim{e|||||||||||||c}h{ûûûûûûûûûû}o{e\\\\\\\\s}earth{speechdefying

empire'sseasons}ravings{e////////x}i{ûûûûûûûûûû}l{e////////s}eternal{riddymravings

bubbleonthecreole}think{c|||||||||||||o}n{ûûûûûûûûûû}t{e|||||||||||||m}vine{continuum,cook

languagesdown}syllable{p\\\\\\\\l}a{ûûûûûûûûûû}t{e\\\\\\\\s}drown{distilledsound

syllablesricochet}tropes{s|||||||||||||i}l{ûûûûûûûûûû}e{n////////t}sense{amongleavescries

curvebetween}shade{g////////e}n{ûûûûûûûûûû}e{r|||||||||||||a}tempo{solidtrunksradiate

strangegrammar}lost{t|||||||||||||i}o{ûûûûûûûûûû}n{s\\\\\\\\o}voice{bubbleatthepotaro

river'smemory}babble{f////////p}l{ûûûûûûûûûû}a{n|||||||||||||t}float{bankgurgle

anaturalhistory}naked{c|||||||||||||y}c{ûûûûûûûûûû}l{e\\\\\\\\s}sense{betweenmossslick

rockswordrides}ravings{b\\\\\\\\l}o{ûûûûûûûûûû}o{d////////i}exiled{riverripples

africvocabulary}green{n|||||||||||||t}h{ûûûûûûûûûû}e{v|||||||||||||i}afterlife{barrelssoverhoarse

falls'roar.rides}sprouts{n////////e}s{ûûûûûûûûûû}x{e\\\\\\\\e}spirit{syntacticsoar

2

yellowblur}ravings{a\\\\\\\\\t}e{ûûûûûûûûûû}i{n////////t}bromeliads{rivershimmer
junglefrondsfurl}green{h|||||||||||||e}m{ûûûûûûûûûû}i{s|||||||||||||t}fronds{dreamsdangle
goldenfrogsstare}tropes{w////////a}f{ûûûûûûûûûû}t{i\\\\\\\\\n}dread{pooleddewripples
waterthunders}unfurl{g|||||||||||||o}v{ûûûûûûûûûû}e{r////////t}voices{birdsflit&zip
lizardsblink}babble{h\\\\\\\\\e}w{ûûûûûûûûûû}a{t|||||||||||||e}gibber{foamcascades
cacophonous}riddim{r|||||||||||||f}a{ûûûûûûûûûû}l{l\\\\\\\\\g}bubbles{spiritlevel
greensphere}ravings{e////////n}e{ûûûûûûûûûû}r{a////////t}rise{arrowheadidea
timeless.creator}green{o|||||||||||||r}o{ûûûûûûûûûû}f{e|||||||||||||l}senses{earth'srockjaw
grindswidegapes}tumble{e\\\\\\\\\c}t{ûûûûûûûûûû}r{i\\\\\\\\\c}exiled{afarfrothingroar
envelopsvegetable}tropes{b|||||||||||||l}o{ûûûûûûûûûû}o{m////////s}froth{kingdomsound
rumblesechoes}blue{c////////r}e{ûûûûûûûûûû}o{l|||||||||||||e}distances{growth'sbustle
empire'sseasons}ravings{e////////x}i{ûûûûûûûûûû}l{e////////s}eternal{riddymravings
bubbleonthecreole}think{c|||||||||||||o}n{ûûûûûûûûûû}t{e|||||||||||||m}vine{continuum,cook
languagesdown}syllable{p\\\\\\\\\l}a{ûûûûûûûûûû}t{e\\\\\\\\\s}drown{distilledsound
syllablesricochet}tropes{s|||||||||||||i}l{ûûûûûûûûûû}e{n////////t}sense{amongleavescries
curvebetween}shade{g////////e}n{ûûûûûûûûûû}e{r|||||||||||||a}tempo{solidtrunksradiate
strangegrammar}lost{t|||||||||||||i}o{ûûûûûûûûûû}n{s\\\\\\\\\o}voice{bubbleatthepotaro
river'smemory}babble{f////////p}l{ûûûûûûûûûû}a{n|||||||||||||t}float{bankgurgle
potarorapidsfume}slide{e////////x}i{ûûûûûûûûûû}l{e|||||||||||||s}cascade{intothegreen
smokefallsupward}riddim{e|||||||||||||v}a{ûûûûûûûûûû}p{o\\\\\\\\\r}sense{kiskadeesmist
yellowblur}ravings{a\\\\\\\\\t}e{ûûûûûûûûûû}i{n////////t}bromeliads{rivershimmer
junglefrondsfurl}green{h|||||||||||||e}m{ûûûûûûûûûû}i{s|||||||||||||t}fronds{dreamsdangle
goldenfrogsstare}tropes{w////////a}f{ûûûûûûûûûû}t{i\\\\\\\\\n}dread{pooleddewripples
waterthunders}unfurl{g|||||||||||||o}v{ûûûûûûûûûû}e{r////////t}voices{birdsflit&zip
orchid.heliconia}drone{m|||||||||||||a}p{ûûûûûûûûûû}m{a////////p}voice{victoriaamazonica
floweringfutures}soaked{c\\\\\\\\\r}e{ûûûûûûûûûû}a{t|||||||||||||e}solar{sepalpetalpistil
stamentongue}riddim{e|||||||||||||c}h{ûûûûûûûûûû}o{e\\\\\\\\\s}earth{speechdefying
empire'sseasons}ravings{e////////x}i{ûûûûûûûûûû}l{e////////s}eternal{riddymravings
bubbleonthecreole}think{c|||||||||||||o}n{ûûûûûûûûûû}t{e|||||||||||||m}vine{continuum,cook
river'smemory}babble{f////////p}l{ûûûûûûûûûû}a{n|||||||||||||t}float{bankgurgle
anaturalhistory}naked{c|||||||||||||y}c{ûûûûûûûûûû}l{e\\\\\\\\\s}sense{betweenmossslick
rockswordrides}ravings{b\\\\\\\\\l}o{ûûûûûûûûûû}o{d////////i}exiled{riverripples

mantra of no return

this piece is / is not about the past, and it is / is not about the future, but it is /
is not about a stasis all waves syncopate. this piece   awash in ways
        is not a pisces, though fish flash in the offing. this piece ripples on the
surface. it foams ashore in futures, it tides back into the passage. these words
shift and chop, dissolve and go nowhere. these words don't go nowhere, they
simply shift atop. they could shift a ship, these words   wharves   shift
and as they do, space shifts, and a ship of some mass also shifts. its contents
shift. its contents constitute a cargo. as with continents, cargo shifts. this piece
is a cargo harried across a world. the cargo constitutes a consonant carried
across. the cargo carries across. this cargo is stars. it is a shifted piece of ass. the
world is itself a cargo carried in the hold of this verse   hold   thoughts
shimmer along pixelated surf. these thoughts are also a cargo. they migrate
without ever arriving at a store. thoughts know no store
     are unsure and sometimes dissemble. economies are unsure and
sometimes dissolve. cargo sinks to the bottom as   shift, overheard.
somewhere in an office, the cargo is written off. the written onus. the letters
crouch and signify in the offing. the signifying mitigates but never ashores.
the arrival is delayed, in four-four tide. the time elects to move forward and
back at once. the tide elects not to arrive but rather to lingo between, among,
within, beneath, atop. the letters syncopate atop the screen but are
backspaced. the   is rewritten

people arrived from portugal. people arrived from africa. people arrived from india. people arrived from england. people arrived from china. people predated arrival. people fled predation. people were arrayed. people populated. whips patterned rays into people. people arose. people rayed outward to toronto, london, boo york. people raided people. people penned the past. people roved over on planes. people talked over people. people rented places. people planted people in people. people raided plantations. people prayed. people re-fried. people died and didn't get second glances. people won scholarships and vanished. people lived atop people. people represented people. people drain-brained. people studied for the common entrance. people paraded. people stumbled and tranced. people took two steps backward. people simmered and boiled over. people plantain. people orphan. people sugarcane. people undocumented. people underground. people never lauded, landed. people arrived but. people   . people departed and arrived again. people retreaded. people stole knowing. people plantation. people horizon. people done run from people. people arrived not knowing their patterns. people arrived riven, alone in the world. people made their way from time. people hailed from climes. people fanned their spreading. people cleaved unto people. people writhed over / under people. people arrived over / under people

"arrive."   two weeks out from election, driving into
georgetown from cheddi jagan international, the roads constrict. a bicycle held
    together by rust, grease, desire, balances. inches fly. the japanese car gears
up, down. inches, or seconds, tick between our engine and an ole
        man, his generation / his sandals thin as the jacket of a penguin classic
            the car swerves, and everyone swerves together. dancehall's two-beat
                        rattles the dash. passengers in the dash, we bide the
same interval, the same interrupt of idle lyricism. what is true is not the poem.
is the rude irruption of the riddim into our pensive longing   blood,
sugar estates combusting   the would-be dictator's bomb that opened
    a hole in rodney   that voiced doom
    into the suburban gardens of retired expats, school headmasters who
weep when the red hibiscus ripples wide and
                        yields its flesh to the yard

we gear into georgetown traffic, brake across latitudes, across martin carter's
"insurgent geographies"   the city's compressed cacophony   echoes
lagos, mumbai, where urgencies converge, simultaneous, improvised
          a goat roped to a post by a ditch and a man burning his trash by the
veer of the road   the schoolchildren filing out of jalousied buildings,
white starched shirts   blown sails above the oceans of navy skirts
    news radio fires: we are two weeks out from election. signs blare their colors
          yellow, green / red, black   checker as neighborhoods flutter
in glass. kokers hang   used guillotines above bled canals. the painted
houses in republic park, their electric gates and razor-wire grin
          boarded stores downtown. the humidity   the pre-election
scream   transmit, and rain's morse responds, deluges us with its
translucent code. cars pull to shoulder. wait, worry drain into the city's gullies,
one meter below sea   level. a tension: granger or ramotar, the invisible
future or the season of the present draws taut across foreheads, around mouths.
a pulse presses out at temples: who will win, the black man or the indian?
what will sprout in this racial cleft   this fusion? the words
          warble, rewind, rain
interjects, rain on the chassis

my mother occupies the passenger seat. my brother and i
            stick in the back.
    the radio babbles and sings between us. she is estranged, returning
         and we are revenants to a place   inside a narration contrived
to read like non-fiction, a continuous telling since   one
mouth inside another, one word emigrating from another's vowels.
    a paper place we've glossed   in novels, in atlases
         materialized into sweltering road   printed under us, the car
horns blasting past, the black faces that map ours for relevance, the faces that
could belong to our relatives   faces we are instructed not to trust, into
whose night we are cautioned against venturing, whose have-not we must not
tempt. my mother banters with the ~~river~~   driver, her voice
angles into   accent, some words chop   others stretch. she ent
home, but her return bends
            here, her speech   soaks into the air near the equator

the rainforest is a mixing board with infinite inputs and infinite outputs.
exponential root strata. riotous snakes. quarter-inch jacks & heads. male /
female. holes and plugs. slithering, electric water. liana cables. bloodvine is a
wire entering, plugging arrival in. line. current will be routed through the
circuit. i am an overproof, alcoholic signal, outbursts clipping. the levels
runneth. hover. kaieteur's torrents kiskadee over. crackle & bloom in the
woofer. georgetown bubbles & skanks tougher. smoke thunder. the old chief
in the canoe gone to his mythmaker. makunaima overlooker. el dorado lover.
destroyer. high wine drifter. black & brown in the fever together. mix it darker.
mix it redder. babylon haunting the jungle swelter.   a tear, amber.
rupununi resistor, a decibel louder. turn up the hemisphere. boost the mighty
rainforest's canopy into the stratosphere. exceed ire. essequibo deliverer.
many rivers branch & spiel, spell black across the atlantic. liquid archive
parser. the wires criscross & the curve is logarithmic. turn the dial on the
mix. haunt the tidalectic. run the console. channel one channel check. spin the
tape, magnetic. warble & flutter. wow & static. increase the gain 'til we overdrive
the terrific. boo. boom a lick. boost the lower end, swell the lower end, theorize
the lower end, occupy the lower end, the 99%, the apocalyptic fundamental
fretting in the bass lean, the nothingness become boeing, becoming

a body, a continental jut

a density of times past

an assemblage of others who are you, a being made of beings
linked down the falls' vertical   down the ribbons of water that
narrow and turn   helices vanish into the emerald   i down who
parents?   down waterfall, down rock, down moss-soft crater, down frond
of the giant bromeliad   down past the abstract   pointillism
of mosquito swarms, down foreign, afar   down the streaming roar
down the curtain of lives, the bustle and drip   leaf folds, moss

grandparents? i pass them on the way down.

they belong to other families   indi-,   akan?

i do not know them.   portu-   chi-?

~~home.~~   new fingerprints form. ferns foam. guyana the
vertiginous   intelligence in whom i am   a cave drawing, a stick
figure holding a bow. a deer flashing into the hush. a moisture of leaves
breathing brown jungle floor.   family hemispheres. arrows scatter. i knew
my great grandmother, and only knew stories of my great grand. counter-
narratives, i don't know any farther, grand, mother, slave, indenture
      i know 2.5 generations, and   i have glimpsed the blistered,
creased photographic evidence. i fall   fermented sugar has spooked the
oral history. the water sings the descent.   the genetic cascade
of the potaro river. power generator. speech distilled in my   and
poured. gold over the lip of the world. in guyana the bloodvines line out,
windward, leeward, radiate, trade routes across a fingerprint

my brother and i stay awake late on the verandah. frogs and crickets zipper, burp, and ripple. our voices surf moist air. we smoke matinées and drink el dorado, then mellow with guinness. a lizard swerves up the wall and clings to the night, upside-down. we itch from mosquito bites, a swarm of red vexations interrupting ease, irritations, the world itching in the meditation

we blow smoke. we discuss who we were before this landing on the continent, before strolling the overgrown botanical gardens haunted by a captive manatee, where teenage love rustles, furtive   the memorial

gazebo with its socialist murals celebrating the workers, how what the leaves hear is not what the roots ask   after one week here questions dissolve, narratives repair, black holes collapse, anxieties evaporate as bullfrog throats rumble. we dissemble. we laugh about being hated, high yellow niggers at home, yet here we are princes, resented, drunk on gold   how the feeling is foreign, baffling, like gagging on money, or guilt from stealing.   nocturnal insects interweave with our breathing, contiguous and shifting, supple, they never stiffen into strict meter, but always evolve. night heaves around us, the entire vegetable kingdom leans in to our verandah to listen

light over den amstel. our purpose here is burial   my uncle didn't care
to weather cold ground, so we have returned to his birthplace, 30 degrees
hotter than the zero of vancouver, his remains in a bamboo urn. wind harasses
the palms. the service swells in a minor key   lace walls loose as music,
breathing, fans dangle from the ceiling, strange shapes of evolution, ineffectually
spinning, elder relatives who remember uncle roger from time   daub
foreheads, faces lustrous, morning blazes to its zenith   once the weeping
song is dry and the sermon spent, we file into the yard. palms flail and bend in
the distance, and an infestation of green interrupts, overgrows the tombs and
headstones, cracks the concrete, bunches between plots, climbs fences, slithers,
multiplies, and now reclines in the ripening day. the trade wind is spiked by
atlantic spray. the mason mixes water and cement, pours and mixes, levels
and smooths, and entombs roger's urn at his grandmother's feet. the concrete
hardens quick in the heat. out front, a pink-and-white hindu temple, an ice
cream sundae, melts across the street.   we arrive with our goodbyes
          shine-faced as currency, we
                              later, we change from slacks and sweating
blazers into pale linens perforated by the breeze, drift to the seawall. under
the vast sweep of brilliant blue   idle-minded, weighted to this unruly
beach whose stones rebuke sandals / reject tourists   we lime, unmoored
     by the departures within

too much has been made of origins
                    all origins are arbitrary
too much has been made of others
                    all others are arbitrary
too much has been made of outbreaks
                    all outbreaks are arbitrary
too much has been made of outcomes
                    all outcomes are arbitrary
too much has been made of outfits
                    all outfits are arbitrary
too much has been made of outlets
                    all outlets are arbitrary
too much has been made of outlines
                    all outlines are arbitrary
too much has been made of outlooks
                    all outlooks are arbitrary
too much has been made of outputs
                    all outputs are arbitrary
too much has been made of outsiders
                    all outsiders are arbitrary
too much has been made of ovens
                    all ovens are arbitrary
too much has been made of owls
                    all owls are arbitrary
too much has been made of owners
                    all owners are arbitrary
too much has been made of ownerships
                    all ownerships are arbitrary
too much has been made of oxygens
                    all oxygens are arbitrary
too much has been made of ozones
                    all ozones are arbitrary

high school fever

nowhere, prairie

all the boys drank.
                        one quarter
lifetime later, have they slouched
        into loving fathers sporting spare tires
husbands assembling dinosaur skeletons
                in two-car garages
        do their sleek heads bob behind the fuzzed
wheels of classic hobby cars, muscle greased, intestines
        squeezed by beltlines, pockets bottomless
into which hands sink and emerge dripping crude
        pumpjacks see-sawing, humping the fever
for high school forever, while obits in the *herald*
        ignored teens from the reserves
who drank themselves to ~~death~~
        to prove their existence, as night wrinkled
                into morning's editorials, in a far flung
suburb of empire, a moneyed slum, a bubble
        born yesterday, a 12-pack of kokanee, a hot piss
filling up an empty, a burp in the back seat, *fast times at ridgemont—*
        skipping in teenage occipital lobes, autobiography
of an outsider screened at the drive-in. nobody
        is in the crashed oldsmobile cutlass supreme, the jaws
of life rend and pry it open   a crumpled tuna can. everybody
        is unconscious, is leaking cheap beer, is stinking
is down by elbow river drinking, listening to creedence
        clearwater revival   or some other
                blue-eyed heresy, disappearing
into the wink of stars between serrated leaves, french
        kissing with cigarette breath, accelerating
legal limit and centrifugal force, steel and glass hurtling
        toward yes, boot in the broken grass, the bloody print
tracked to this nowhere, this prairie, this periphery, this intoxicated
        accident   blackout into this suburb

blundering out of time, this shithole built by bitumen, this fort
    where raw tobacco, chili peppers, alcohol were stirred
in the bottom of a barrel, where gunpowder and fire-water
    were served, this inflamed adolescence of the human experience
at the saddledome, at the hockey game, in don
    cherry's swollen pituitary grandstand, in between periods, in between
vaseline and sperm-slick fingers under the covers, i was the only
    boy who did not dream of sex with the stanley cup, but of suicide
in the back seat, breathing carbon monoxide as *exodus*
    sang my body into the emptiness above the dust
and yellow grass, the gopher holes and hot asphalt, up
    over the foothills and rockies, out of these suburbs of

        brome grass
trespasses into my home in the city
        a flat plain of golden green
rolls through the window. the grass
        curves under the wind. blue widens above.
a single ripped cloud surrenders
        and slinks away. the prairie sprawls forever
until, at its very edge, it drops off a cliff
        and there at the bottom
lie phantom bones translucent in the sun. the prairie repeats
        through these letters, it travels from nowhere
to nowhere, like a poem, from one age to another
        over which, maybe, the cowboy flunkies will—
like a chinook. mournful. really, i don't know
        anything about the prairies i just grew
up there, i don't feel sentimental
        about brome grass, country music, seed catalogues
midnight meteor showers screened on the big sky, although somehow
        sedans from the 1980s make me weep, sentimentally
a chaperoned slow-dance in the school gym
        that defies sincerity, because
i am no longer fun, or young, or drinking a king can
        in a field off elbow drive, or screwing
in a parent's company car, a lincoln continental
        oldsmobile cutlass supreme, big caddy
brown buick regal with gold trim, burgundy
        town car gleaming sweet and eternal
as rage, as a first electric touch of pussy, as a dying high
        i want to recline
in velour upholstery in a parking lot by the river, flick on
        darkness, extinguish the music, and in the soft nowhere
under the poplar trees, hot box
        until the air is   white waves under the windows,

wafting up the glass, and we are submerged, and we
    lose consciousness as the river churns us
into our 4th decade, the car a junked memory
    that doesn't turn over, sunk to the bottom of the gone never
ever again, goodbye, and i am in my home
    dumb among all i own, in a strange city at midnight
maple trees out the window, cool rippled
    laughter, cigarette smoke, and french
whose speakers don't give a shit about john ware,
    the black cowboy, or teenage auto-erotic
asphyxiation that ended in unintentional
    suicide, circa 1990
or me.

these were the worst years of my life. i wasn't supposed to admit that. my
guidance counselor admonished my boner. nancy reagan worried the war on
drugs. we were all suburban zombies haunting b-movies rented at the strip-
mall. the video store hid an adult section in the rear, behind western doors. i
hated, bullied, bucked. i wanted to be certain, i wanted to be heterosexual and
popular, not a black cretin. i smoked weed behind the generator behind the
tennis bubble. i wanted to eat pink panties. i confessed nothing and stole
money. i wanted to asphyxiate during my orgasm, but instead wept after i
jerked myself. my teachers called me a liar. i wrote the word **f-u-c-k** on the
wall. i was supposed to be a follower, a wallflower, to squeeze a football while
wearing only a jock-strap, but the ethnic tension was too elastic. i cringed
through 78 days of oka and then desert storm. the flung stones shattered car
windows, and yahoos strutted. i watched the news in the basement on the
corduroy couch. i snuck alcohol. the students chanted U-S-A! U-S-A! in the
parking lot behind the school. i remember yasser arafat's fatigues, his keffiyeh
wrapped around his head. i dipped copenhagen, red man chaw, and vomited.
my saliva blackened as my mouth soured. i measured my erection with a
yellow plastic ruler, which i stole from elementary school. i buckled under
apartheid and *dance me outside*, which i read three times before i had any
pubic hair, or politics. sadie one-wound, silas ermineskin, frank fencepost,
the poor girl murdered amid all of the alcohol and racism. all of that laughter
at whose expense? who is going to get bashed tonight? whose button fly will
get yanked open while the blood throbs in our frontal lobes? who will puke
the peach schnapps, its surging sweetness burning throats, bullying to avoid
being bullied, always wanting a shower and never guessing that these sour
bowels make us human. i shivered in the evangelical rupture of the suburbs.
the good samaritan shouted down his wife. his sermon boomed outside his
home, shattered windows, burst door hinges. the older boys skateboarded
and smoked export in the parking lot of mac's. they were no better than apes,
but their parents pretended. my brother wore a kente-cloth cap and a free

mandela medallion. i wore jeans and scrapped. the adults looked down their noses. our currency was shit-mixes in mason jars and stolen cigarettes smoked in garages. i felt dirty. everyone was scowling at me. i showered and fantasized about the boys in my class. naked thighs and penis. i obsessed over sex, i sucked sensation from joints of hash. the white girls were taunting, unattainable. the black, brown, beige ones were invisible. i was nowhere, calgary was nowhere. none of the dark girls smouldered on the magazine covers at red rooster. i bought slurpees and poured in vodka then fell asleep playing ms. pac-man in the middle of the bad years. everyone hated me. everyone was from some hayseed backwater in saskatchewan. their children were blonde, spoiled, and unlovable. i was spoiled and unlovable. i wanted freckles. i despised freckles. apoplectic fits, orgasms, spankings in the unfinished basements.

one quarter lifetime later, the captain of the football team walks
        into a sitcom. his name is norm. the sunshine girl is a mom.
            the hockey players
who died in that crash after the barn burner in okotoks are unknown
        to the internet. high school was a three-year fever
that consumed the prairie, one long wet dream
        subsidized by the oil and gas industry. every day a gusher
of slurs, a profane well deepened and pumped in the minds
        of the future, while some teen sobbed in a bathroom stall
the words: *kilroy was here*   scraped into the door
        above him, a cartoon thought-bubble, a caption—
shunned, desperate for a vehicle, an oldsmobile more
        expensive than his teacher's, whose students all learned:
it's a small, material world, learned algebra,
        life-skills, social studies, typing, lying, how to finger-fuck
and to squirm and curdle   after all,
some evangelical couple's freckled son
        will confess a gay fantasy to a guidance counselor
whose corduroy suit stinks of smoke, old coffee, and rum, then
        will hang himself in his parents' home after he plummets
from an ejaculation in the locker room. the whole
        neighborhood will vote reform. the whole neighborhood
will lose the remote control. the whole neighborhood
        will pray to wayne gretzky while singing the national anthem
and will then grease white jesus' bum.
        do you see what i mean? it's friday
the 13th. part 666. i am irrational.
        i am crushed between the canines
of my anger. i am a fleeing, hysterical fool
        in a slasher flick. if my eyes flicker back
over my shudder, toward the past,
        i'll pause the VHS—

cross-legged in front of the chrome
akai hifi   i sipped hashish smoke. plugged
    the coiled cable into the jack—
        planted my head in the phones

the cruiser arrived at the station,
police opened the car door and Griffin attempted to flee

their black mouths opened over my ears
    transfixed me with their holy warble in tongues

two police officers picked Mr. Stonechild up
for creating a disturbance. Four days later

the cassette clicked and spun, this communion with slowed
    magnetic sound my salvation, sound tongued my auricle

outraged that a young black man
could be fatally shot while complying

in a slow vertiginous whorl, an analog machine speaking in cyclic stereo
    my cranium was covered in electric needles that reached

the Saskatoon police department
preferred not to know what happened

up through the hole in the ozone layer. the singer's patois
    leaped between poles of plutonian midnight winter

a white mob in Lasalle stoned a convoy of Mohawks
mostly women, children

and the unconcious house, the snow burning, the winter moon a haze of heat
  an amplifier's bulb overdriven, melting night

his body was found with just one shoe on;
he had frozen to death on the outskirts

my eyelids low against the glow, green lashes casting shade
  over white sub-zero dunes, flakes spiraling down from the stucco

seniors leaving Kahnawake for what they had hoped would be safety,
amid rumours of an impending

ceiling, through a waking dream of being nothing, being a void

ordered to stop or risk being shot. He complied
with the order and turned around. Seconds later

an empty body in which smoke, blue reverberation, and ash float

inside the music was a hiss, the hiss of hash smoke released by heat, the hiss of
3M tape riding a slow reel   the ambient release of doubt in the darkened
half of the brain, the dust and static crackling, a hiss that engulfed the sound

   a hiss that became a white roar, cloud or air or smoke drubbing inside
me, inside of which there must have been a door   inside the cascading
foam of kaieteur   analog memory become white noise

   density of whispers in both ears, this   my thesis, there must have
been a door inside somewhere   if i could pass through   and
find myself in the past   but the whispered babble dropped into a
rumble   a pattern, a bassline that skanked froth   and locked with a
drum's low kick—maybe the drum's black period was—   but the door was
closed, and the music took shape again, mobile architecture lighter than air

   brass wafting over the cyclic song, and i listening, feeling almost—found

   i'd almost reached through no return to touch   but there was
nothing there, only space, an ever-receding gleam, the dying luminosity of
alpha centauri, winked out of existence like species, but still lingering in the
onyx

   drip of a dream, maybe. i was dreaming. maybe? the smoke swirled to a
drop, the skeletal sound a supple graph of notes, of pure time and form

   steady on the air   i am 400 years from home, with
stardust and salt mixing in my rizla. high   by the mute dials'
nocturnal fizzle

i hold a hyphen between my fingers.   divining rod   strains
          recurring dream of verandahs, crickets in the dusk   beacons
                    flocks of vowels and consonants migrating along the creole
continuum, from one grammar into another   one place into another,
another yard shimmers   a curtain of beaded raindrops
     memory monsoon. we reach through   to touch who is reaching toward us
                    simultaneous, neither othered nor halved   but
whole   reconciled?   questions: how can a place that's
absent be more prescient than one that is   how
          wait   can a thought be unbounded territory can a person live in a
particular place for 20 years yet only be "in" and not "of" that
          vernacular   how can a person return to the place they are "from" yet
suddenly realize   the stereo is on

exploding radio

an abandoned radio's static roars against the ocean

walking the seawall   thought and noise converge in a needle
shivering between stations. having traversed air, am i noise or am i here?

how can i return somewhere i've never been?

seeker, descendent, returnee, one who
was once abducted and has now fled

am i visiting or being visited? do i possess the vocabulary of
discovery or does it possess me?   is this a cliché

working to recover myself from infiltration by the culture of empire

over the folding waves   overlapping flight patterns, frigate
wings, coasting   territories

an exxon rig crouches offshore

at home in montréal three springs later, time collapsed, the city
melting, my potted palm fronds sere in the electric air, i stare over the open
book: *cahier d'un retour . . .*   out the window: ocean

pacing. on the seawall, poised to receive some revelation   sucked, as
the tide seeps and gurgles   i walk the wall, the squat wave splinterer,
concrete city limn, as it curves with the continent   a long stone
sentence that chronicles the dissolution of city into plastic bags, cereal boxes,
torn wrappers, ribbed aluminum sand   ripped envelopes   fine crushed
glass into windrush, no terminus, diaspora folds and unfolds   the lines
bend both ways   sand burns in each worn, directionless crease, and
we are heaved up with the   world's jetsam: bleach bottles,
styrofoam balls, beer cans   feet on the continent's tectonic edge, the
ridge above the plastic beach, i stare north to where sky and water, silver
and brown, fuse in an incandescent meeting of cloud and spray, fuse in a
consipiratorial line   those who made the middle
passage   could not see back across
the question. the calm ocean must have seemed a chasm. the white gulls

writing in air, indifferent historians. the hot population   commodity,
or carrion.   i turn my back to the vexing   to the ocean.

    to the south, black cricketers in starched whites strike bat against ball
& sprint the pitch. they squint against the circular flare in the ozone. somewhere,
the tin treble of the radio studs the noonday   heat stammers down

descended, in part, from a continent shaped like a question mark
descended, in part, from those who were sold

descended, in part, from those indentured
descended, in part, from those who rebelled

descended, in part, from charles tanner-lam
of hong kong, migrant to guyana circa 18-o-long

descended, in part, from those who bought and owned others
descended, in part, from a question mark—

perhaps arawak, perhaps indian, perhaps
portuguese, perhaps english, i don't know

how not to be multiple. i don't know
what to desire from this avowal.

i listen for a word, a welcome, but the ocean
kisses its foaming teeth and tosses its head

its pressed curls twirl in style, show its snub,
show its art. did i expect

to be addressed? no sudden solar flare
ignites a blood understanding.

back into the septic atlantic
that flattens as it extends to the horizon

nothing is my meditation. nothing is a radio
with antennae raised, its cheap speakers' tinned

ping, noise surging in a curled conch, or a voice
hollowed in bone. gulls, pinned to the edge of the wind

sing single notes, big tankers float,
their bulk resonant, drums, their engines

shiver through the chopped water, up the shore
not in even measure, but staggering, ructious, irate, dispatching

aftershocks through the city's asphalt. the ships
swell at anchor, hands cupped to receive a cargo

of bauxite, lumber, labor, drugs bound for another
accounting that sums

elsewhere, beyond this local preface to privation. paradise
ripening in frustration, the swollen ships angle

toward port of spain, miami, new york, kingston
havana, montréal, vancouver

here, on this continent, what of black versus brown, fratricidal
quadrille rung on the steel oil drum, what of

prime minister burnham's eye,
the bomb his men rigged

to blow rodney silent, blow a hole in the walkie-talkie
announcing its dry spark

across savannah,
its crackle hurried on fm frequencies

the non-aligned nations fallen
into static, into phalanx with the cubans, the vietnamese

clamoring that class is not ingrained
in skin, in color, in black at the bottom

red in the middle, and gold close enough
to join the local elite: trujillo, papa / baby doc, pinochet

the red
comrades, usurping

menace adrift on the mute breeze. a hint
of authoritarian dynamite

ticking under the topos. the open ocean discloses
nothing. trafficking. where is my dread

welcome? where my fatigues
my locks, my beard, my non-aligned rifle? where

is my revolution?

1980. i was 5 in a carpeted bungalow in vancouver. my mother used to take me
to ambleside beach at low tide to turn over rocks in search of translucent

crabs. viscous sea moss and wet sand, anemones anchored,
the pacific ocean cold. 1980

drops

into darkness. outside

georgetown prison
the car radio playing, song

soft over the grumble of internal combustion
rodney's heart speeding as he glances

at shadows, slowing as he settles back
into the night's unhurried breath

drone, chirrup, rustle, groan, gurgle rippling
in concentric arcs from no center, expanding everywhere

converging on this car parked, on this body,
dispersing through the circuit of veins and synapses, nerve impulses

firing through flesh, and reverberating back into
everything living

frog flitting beneath the dew-darkened
leaves, everything living, in rhythm, everything

breathing with everything, and then—

and then—a

spark, a

rip in the peace of the universe

and blooming fire expanding   blasting the living

blowing car window   shards

to pierce hearts   pierce hopes

wound the future   the bursting spark flare

out against the night and ignite

death and the radio x-   plode the dark, voices scatter like

fireflies, like o

bright birds aflame, o   voices flung

o   pain buzzing stinging the tropical blackness

o   static crack / crick and scatter, soundwave snakes, shockwaves verbing

o   screaming through the skeletal moon glow, screaming holes

o   holes blown in the chassis, in the man heself, in the air in time, in the word love

and the city boomed awake to shuddering

o   burning o weeping o wailing o pressure o

all time stop.

1980. drop

and smoke

in columns from the broken. blaze up to cure the moon.

now through this hole in the truth, radio demerara firing out and reloading
a bulletin framing this man, this historian, this rodney of flesh and black
and continental afro of tanzanian memory, behind horn-rimmed spectacles
the fashion   bell bottom'd for his own heart's rupture   and a melody
drifts along the smoke but only troops rush in, and another verdant day
flares as the radio exports: "from buxton on the east coast to the church of
the immaculate conception"

the funeral procession

come, mourners walking on air

footfalls soundless, earth

open, broken, ready to receive

a breaker hurls its head against this vancouver beach, hammering rocks

white foam hissing and scattering up

walking the seawall. a figure walks toward me
balanced on the gray

boundary, she steps into focus and we cross
parallels, i recognize her from the flight. she mirrors me

our echoing accents, our doppled displacement, our winter
attuned, pitched in our greeting

homing,
we meet in airports, on outskirts

along the seam between worlds
she is my context

returning after 30 years, and i am hers
at 39 visiting for the first time. my aunt saunters over

& we three become a ~~nation~~: black, mixed, indian
without a flag to wave, without an anthem, foreign attrition

we rationalize distance: family, job, money, the voylence after sundown
overgrown, trash-strewn

words freighted with estrangement and guilt, we toss them out
and burn them between us. smoke

of our emigrant ceremony, our crossing of pasts, we depart
opposite, along the sentence that encircles the world

i stand on the seawall staring over the plastic
beach that slides under the tide

jet engines will soon launch me over the dun
atlantic, and before i can adjust my tongue,

i'll be sweating on a bus in june
in a speckled rush-hour crowd

with tight french vowels tickling the ear
staring out the window at concrete and traffic

montréal, and an ache to return will surge and pulse as the veined
routes that hold

hard   my dumb magnetic dub   blood's tide will shift
that radio in the worn gazebo nailing its beat into noon

sweating minutes, buckling continent, vault of water groaning as the planet rolls
and the cheap speakers thud time in

bullfrogs and crickets, the forest steaming with quiet slow breaths
digesting itself, ruminating on its green as i sit in the present, this northern

city with its concrete teeth grinding everything
to letters and dist—

bow

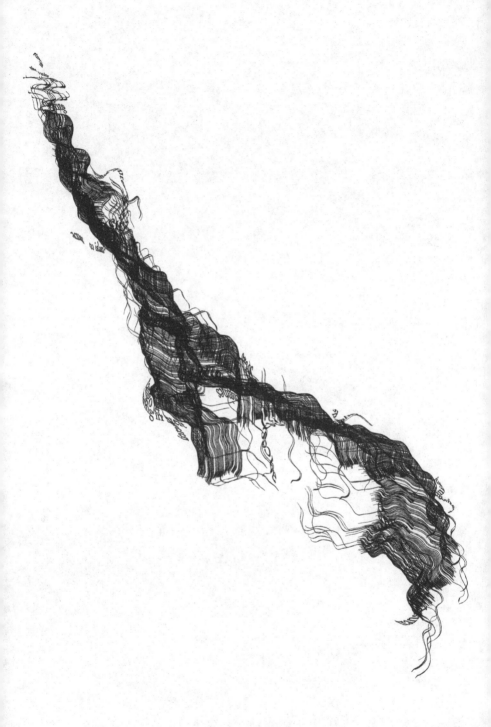

zero degrees

smoke	eddies, slinks along the stucco ceiling
smoke	dispersed by a slow hand
smoke	weightless as bass
smoke	braids into the fibers of winter sweaters
smoke	saturates the air and suffocates
smoke	settles around us like fur, or spirits
smoke	lucent in the sunlight, mist over morning
smoke	inhaled and held in the alveoli, it can't be grasped by a hand
smoke	swells, silvers, rolls lethargic and slow
smoke	its striations swim in the light and rise like flooded rivers
smoke	stains the filter, yellows the index
smoke	sweet and white, sizzles off the cherry
smoke	the zeitgeist. it permeates pores, cells, cultures
smoke	coils round our fingers, inhales us, binds us to this act
smoke	slithers off the hot knives heated in the stove's glowing coils
smoke	a quiet high, a cancer
smoke	pours out of lévesque's nostrils the night of the long knives
smoke	travels in a solid column, unbreathable as water
smoke	cascades through the crack in the car window
smoke	exhaled from the exhaust pipe, pumped out by the engine's muffled chug
smoke	billows inside the rubber tube that runs from the exhaust to the window
smoke	tumbles upward through the tube and vomits its fog into the car
smoke	erases the face of the boy unconscious in the back seat
smoke	sneaks into his nostrils, slinks down his throat
smoke	thickens into a white confusion
smoke	an airtight seal around the brain
smoke	cotton plugging his mouth and nose
smoke	chokes him, wakes him, wraps him, holds its hand over his mouth
smoke	clouds his lidded pupils, whispers nothing, nothing, nothing

1. take old newspapers: the *calgary herald*, the *globe and mail*
2. take scotch tape
3. take rubber tubing, black, coiled in a suburban garage
4. take a roll of duct tape
5. take a bottle of extra-strength tylenol
6. take another bottle, gravol
7. take a mickey of demerara rum
8. take pen and paper
9. take a cassette: *exodus*, to jam into the deck
10. take all of this that nobody will miss, that your parents might only notice months after you've taken yourself from them, and when they do—

sit in the basement. write that this taking is not fair, it is selfish and final, it produces no reciprocal act. it gives nothing. your mother reminds you that she and your father give and give, and you take and take, and this is the final taking. in this taking of yourself from everyone else, from parents who conceived without consulting you, conceived you from swirling stardust, water, and air, elements to which you wish to return, you take yourself from all of the little agonies that conspire to take you over, you take yourself from being into nothingness, and you give yourself elemental dispersal. all of the people who feel that you belong to them will feel as if you have been taken from them: an agonized emptiness, a rent in the earth. you will be gone, given over to your terminal taking now that the accessories have been enumerated, what should you wear? a favorite outfit? something comfortable, not confining? something that puts the mind at ease and allows you to forget yourself while you embrace your dying

now that the outfit has been selected, the faded levis, the black all stars with the broken canvas, the rumpled t-shirt lettered with the name of a skateboard company, the yankees baseball cap with the curved brim to yank down over your eyes, a shade to blot out the audience and any future act beyond this one

now that the newsprint has been duct-taped over the windows on either side of the garage, you step back and look at how the sunlight tries to peer through the paper, lightening the pages from gray to flax, and how the garage glows, and you wonder at the innocence of newsprint, life's narratives typeset upside-down, sideways, how the neighbors won't notice anything, not even the quotidian crises, the idle horrors it announces

now that the rubber tube has been duct-taped to the exhaust pipe, run around the side of the car and up into the rear window, the window has been rolled as high as it will go to clench the tube between its tip and the chrome frame—airtight but for two inches now that newsprint has been taped over those open two inches, two layers of fine print, two layers of pulp you will never have to inhale again

now that you have swallowed half the bottle of tylenol and the rum is pounding in your chest, in your eardrums, in your neck, at your temples

now that the key is in the ignition

now that the engine stutters, rumbles, and drones

now that you have lain down in the back seat, the cassette clicks and begins its slow spin, the album *exodus*. as the band sings and soars, you sink into the silver upholstery of the oldsmobile cutlass supreme, into the softness of the suburbs, the fuzz of tylenol and carbon monoxide that bleaches the air in the car. the interior is white, impenetrable with engine exhaust. you think about what you want to write. you want to explain, but then you don't. you want to lash out, scrawl, dismiss life as a decision forced upon you. how do you begin. you close your eyes and think, and the thought drips from your limp fingers. the page   if anyone were to look in the window they would not see the boy lolling in the back seat. the air is dense, unbreathable, but the body still heaves. its biology drives it to   . this is its will. it shudders as it gulps   the music   the wailers band rides their upbeat skank, rides their pneumatic bassline through the analog cloud, a mystic song that stalled   breath can't silence, delivering its message even as a shadow crowds the cranium   a high, hoarse wail piercing the engine's numbing hum, a voice suffused with sorrow and rage refuting sleep, scorning resignation, singing your self up, up out of the car, out of the darkened garage and toward the brilliance that explodes into shards and pierces pupils, stinging you back into sunlight and leaf

the truth?
is the white cursive issued from a brick chimney
is a skeleton in brown gabardine
wandering the underground city, an accent
adrift in its second language
over a b-side version of empire
i speak french. i am a sovereign state drifter
winter hinterlander with a mortgage
and expired aeroplan points, a vacation blazing
on the credit line
unnecessary to history, my culture extracurricular
creole vernacular stutterer, i ride the metro
underground with my fur
collar tickling my chatter, metro shuttle station to station,
but i don't matter, carapace of white earbuds contains my rude—
redemption, i go to work in the heart of a conquered
devotion, a thin mist descends over me
a blown surrender,
snow falls through me. it is always snowing inside me.
my hand is a blue *fleur-de-lys* torched by autumn
my sap is slow, it hardens glistening in its circuit,
the sharpness of pine and spruce tingles
on the yellow edge of my breath
i find refuge from winter in the hudson's bay
boxing day sale. born in a corporation, i can't pretend,
i was not born on the equator,
i died in the upholstered ease of a sedan, and here is my after, city blistered
gray by salt and winter, work in a tower, a payment plan carrying anonymous
class aspirations, and this
is my squalor, an abstract longing to cruise the foothills in a lincoln continental
hearse, bleached teeth chattering nonsense as the zero of winter ascends

one tectonic plate buckled under another, mountains. i have heard my
relatives say they don't want to be buried in the cold ground   a refutation of
this place where they have wintered, years, a refutation of their own refusal
here, a double negative, a final rebuke to issue, a final no, i refuse you who
refused me, forever. stern confirmation that they must be laid to rest in the
south american soil near the turning equator. this makes sense to me. this
refusal, this remove, that they do not want this discriminating earth, that
you can't own me forever   we sealed my uncle's ashes in their bamboo urn.
after the disruptions of flight and customs, the jostling   sweating, the
rumpled linen, the searches and questions, the delays   the bewildered
eruptions, the rattling bone fragments, we planted his ashes in a green
eternity, palms flinging their locks against burnished cobalt   out
     past the church gate, a curious goat roped to a stake at the dirt
crossroads, the pastel ice cream concrete softening toward siesta, fronds
lolling on the moist air   uncle roger's spirit could choose to rest or
wander down one asplahlt stretch and up another, gravel and dirt, until he
reach the ocean, lime   read the extended lines of cursive foaming on
brown, surging to shore, double-spaced   phalanxes of diaphanous prose

the palimpsest of the prairie   its bearded wheatgrass might have
nodded to the rhythm of the king james   wind's transparent wave riding
blonde grass, invisible ink sweeping over the recursive curve, no detail of my
life written in the narrows between the blades   i never cared to be a
pastoral poet, or a poet of small flatland longings, a poet of evangelical strictures,
of social discredit, fire and brimstone apoplexies   but of equatorial
revolutions, oceanic futures written in the veins of the vegetal

   tenements of babel dense with voices, languages spilling out the summer
windows onto the basketball-drubbed asphalt of little burgundy, montréal
the palimpsest city, one game played over another, one culture settled over
another, english spoken over créole spoken over french over each tenant a
turned page in each apartment, each apartment the idea of an island,
repeating upward 20 storeys, créole meltdowns simmering, pepperpot
sweating in those horizontal tenements that stacked and shipped my
ancestors across to islands, to new south american savannahs, new rivers,
new langugaes, new words fluttering in the mouth

turbulence in a blue tango jet, buffeted by cloud, engines roaming in stereo, pursuing the logic of better mus come   landing on this denuded, sparkling hinterland, flat slab of earth, before driving the long expressway in from the airport, crossing the bow river waiting in line for culture, another year

                    barely inching forward. in the semi-basement barbershop in a northeast strip mall, low rent drop-ceiling and no cash register, next to speedy muffler, listening to dated dancehall hits, beenie man's slack stammer-simmer, thinking man this is fucking nowhere, prairie nowhere, terminal starlight tour, is this a beginning or a layover or

turning back, is this a beginning?   is it preferable to be erased, to have a
voice that does not know the chorus because it sounds outside the tradition,
because it is stolen by the chinook, or to have a dream of sweating in the
malarial mud swarmed by *morpho peleides*, sapphire butterflies, each one the
spirit of an ancestor   is it better to own a new bungalow in a
new development, or to live where your name was born, where your memory
has tongue   is this the reckoning: being between, turning between a
newness of mr. clean and president's choice, and choke-and-rob in the bloody
dusk, between a full tank of gas and love in a time of bauxite strikes   i have
to reckon with this far reach, this far flung, this beyond beyond the
perimeter, wandering latitudes of longing and ache, where there exists no
critical authentic, no mas, nothing but blown fragments, and a polaroid
            frozen at the departure gate, timehri in 1973.   i look up from my
aunt's afro.   out the sedan's window: mile markers, flashing fenceposts and
barb wire slung between

clouds, unconscious in their blind dreaming   the prairies stretch beyond
death, baffle the compass   earthen tongues ripple speechless under dead
air, weightless volume of big sky   the foothills, humpbacked brown
leviathan, surface and plunge   a volcanic hollow   *une coulée de*
pensées, une coulée de lettres, une coulée de lave   the athabasca glacier
recedes into prehistory, dinosaur ice trickling into time's crystalline wink
     reception weakening the further we   from the city, clear static
between stations, mountains as ancestors, blue teeth to the sun
     history the complex of freedom and catastrophe, the found, the
concrete, the territory   on the prairies the lanes move   the lines shift,
narrative swerves under cloud changing shape like a thought   i am the
merest vehicle, great engine of tongues babbling toward a still point   a giant
period blackly riding the hills' humped complexities, patterns beneath the
formulaic speech   the attempt to unite landscape and immortality
     talking to defeat direction   the pleasure of departure   the
vexation of return   the road like a dream, out of the dark into the
struggle   the new morning so barren   furious outsider wandering
the edge of the river valley   the whooping cranes that mate for life
     the tyranny of this stolen narrative   the fields of grain shift

ghost notes

the author's voice drones   harmonizes with the room's ambient hum

    fuses with the electric zzzzzzzzzzzzzzzzzzzzzzzzzzzzz amplified by a
ventilation shaft, its sawtooth wave climbs a door-frame, bores into ceiling
panels   vibrates down to linoleum and rebounds up femurs, tibias,
spinal columns, spirals into cranial orifices & drones on   a boy who
does not belong in this faculty, in this book, in this time or place, who should
not be remembered, stands and asks the mannered, middle-aged authors
about writing and place, and whether they write from place   about
place, to place, whether their sentences subsist against snow and suffer
migraines when the chinook arches its cloud-rippled dome airtight, shut over
the drive-ins of southwestern alberta, whether their lives are bounded by a
reserve or by the trembling, rickety wooden homes that stagger around
victoria park, skid row in the saddledome's shadow

autumn 15 years later, without answer, he is speeding
seated, shot on a chrome greyhound
       through golden farmlands at sunset, pink
and orange beams streaming between leaves
       scattering shadows across the directionless
              flatness   an asphalt strip
divides the foothills, drives forward and back
       between pasts and futures, wow and flutters
thru towns inhabited by baseball caps and
       plaid shirts, by tim hortons, by belt-buckles
clinked locked above zippered wranglers, by ford
       pickups raising dust on old-boy back roads, abandoned
barns angled with the wind, cowboy hats adrift atop
       the rye grasses, fence posts bound by barb wire
wooden churches whose doors open onto fire
       and boredom   i was wondering whether your writing
is haunted by place, does place matter
       do your letters inhabit locales –
the writers circumnavigate the question
       with smiles and gestures that dismiss, they write
from everywhere at once, or from nowhere exactly, and the only
       place is the imagination, the immediate port at which the next letter
arrives, is detained, or vanishes, the imagination exists neither
       here nor there, is everywhere, which is here, which is
nowhere. the letters rush into the black dipper
       the great cipher of our gaping television sets, they come from nowhere
they ride the wheel of fortune, the price is irrelevant because
       an oil well bubbles in our backyards
here is nothing   but letters like constellations that predate
       suburbs and belong to no one, they simply exist and multiply in spite
of no cluster of skyscrapers in the center of no city, no round tower
       revolving at the center of no still burbs, no bungalows stretching flatly

no foothills, no stupid mute sky yawning into no solar system
      no specific context for our living, our violence, just the words
suspended, turning in the sharp air   i think differently
      in montréal from how i did in calgary, i write and dream
in georgetown guyana with a flying fish
      carried on the frothed surge of a thought, a heron
hunting iguana amid low bush, a god folded into the body
      of a golden frog squatting in a puddle of dew
at the heart of a giant bromeliad, two marble eyes beaming
      creation into my electric cortex, my skull
a satellite dish in the backyard, curved and wondering
      curved and receiving, a cup to catch abundance, a screen
flickering at the drive-in, a pale yawn   waiting for a close encounter from

i'd like to erase this poem. i'd like to erase the syntax i grew up in: the
unlettered suburbs, the strip malls, the pickup trucks   the spilled asphalt,
the ranchers and bungalows, the clustered skyscrapers exclaiming downtown,
the futurist signifying of the calgary tower   i would leave the natural
grammar: the bow river, the supple foothills that accelerate as they buckle
into sawtooth peaks that scrape the big sky   i can't erase everything, so i
choose to erase myself, remove myself from the prairie come the 1980s, gulping
white exhaust in the garage, or on a blurred silver greyhound   fleeing the
province to vanish into anonymous eastern multitudes, a slow smudging that
only a poem's time-lapse lettering can

there was the 60-something man with the nicotine-streaked beard who
there was the businessman on the city bus, drunk after work, who
there were the yahoos down at the stampede grounds who
there were the co-workers in canmore who
there were the older boys at school who
there were the reform politicians who
there was the librarian who wouldn't let me check out books until my mother
exploded. there were the teachers who forced us to our knees and demanded to
know if we had brains under our afros. there were the clerks, cops, and security
guards who haunted us as we spooked the city. there were the suspicious
glances, the surreptitious glares, the undisguised disgusted looks. there was
the muttered nigger, the shouted nigger, the whispered nigger, nigger spoken
at casual conversational volume, nigger at measured intervals, the ethiopian
famine as punch line, basketball teams raping white women as punch line,
curry oozing from pores, the reductive tropes, the weaponized hilarity and
negative reinforcements, the rejections in the lineup for the bar, the police who
there was the absence of
there were the remarks that
there were the co-workers who
there was the clerk at the bay who
there were the parents of friends who
there was the librarian at the public library who
there were the mothers in the neighborhood who

we were children. we were teenagers. we were trying to outgrow sliced
forearms, nooses in winter garages, weed-smoke frozen in the air,
submergences under the ice that covers the glenmore reservoir, howling
emergencies to which no one responds, furious alcoholics who outgrow their
addictions at 40, or later, or never, faces bloated, who need rum to silence the
voice that refuses to stop whispering that they are nothing, shit, failure,
degradation, that they will not get the job, that they will rot from the inside
out, not make the team, that their idea sounds better coming from thinner
lips, that they are a thief, a suspect, an interloper, a porter and that they
should forever remain proud of this, a fugitive janitor, a cipher who arrived
north of the border naked ahead of a pack of dog-headed men, a severed
penis crammed into its owner's mouth, an intermittent signal that flickers in
and out of reception, a nether presence, a foul odor issued from a void, a
shoeless shoe-shine boy, a black beetle with a hard back, an insect to be
crushed underfoot, a remedial student, a "fucking retard," a clown in the rear
of the class, an ape, a thug, a base species devolved from ignorance, an anus, a
basehead, an omission, a thing incapable of thought and to be communicated
with by profanity and screaming, a black morass, insult, jungle-bunny, curry-
eater, nigger, a wrong racist slur applied, regurgitation, a low beast to batter
with shouts and truncheon-blows, a zombie, a rotting clump of flesh, a
monstrosity leering forth from the mirror, a virulent plague infecting the
city, against which blonde girls must be inoculated, a lung to be inflated with
smoke, threat of threats, once you go black you'll never find the door of no
return, an ominous dildo, a brainless body owned by an inferior,
supermasculine menial, property of another, an unwanted buck, a prowler
who materializes at night, a steel-wool-headed criminal, burr for brains,
breath stinking like cumin, a dismissive, flippant line in a literary work: the
impenetrable musk of the negro, a tragic mulatto, a corsair, a heart of
darkness, an inscrutable swamp behind the eyes, blackamoor, a white-
toothed bug-eyed shakespearean murderer in a jealous rage, a brute crawling

among swine and plunging lips into a filthy feeding trough, a fucking animal loose in the elementary school, in the junior high school, in the shopping mall, a back to be flogged until the skin rips and bloodies   this is your superior profanity. this is what we leave behind when we tumble off the toilet in a stupor. this is why we depart for toronto and montréal, what we swear to never turn back to. this is what exists in the rear of our short-circuited classroom, all of it behind the ears like so much decomposition, raw sewage oozing from our fizzling, blackened cortex toward our ha

the writing junks apart like a rust-gnawed camaro parked in a prairie field,
scoured by the bald sun, pierced by a thousand grass spears flung up from
the center of the earth nature's upward thrust slicing steel   the letters
somersault   buffalo cascading over a cliff, legs pumping in air, falling
with the lost demerara boy who stung his senses with white lightning and
stumbled off the prairie's edge hoping   to tumble through space and
splash into the potaro, the essequibo, kaieteur's torrents hanging spume
flecking blue and flying upward, a watery rewind to the dawn of his
consciousness cradled in the forest's folio   the golden frog concealed in
the pooled dew in the branching green frond of the giant bromeliad, watching
          i don't know where i am in this writing, in this liquid page where the
poem dissolves into molten gold and pours over a cliff   which isn't a
poem, and i never could write one, and i don't want to ever be able to do that,
because it would mean writing in the wrong tradition, alongside those who
segregated anthologies, internalizing their derision, flattering a world shrunk
to the contour of their cerebral convolutions, and no, i am not them, i am the
not-them who abides inside all they elide, i am not in their vocabulary, there
exists no known tongue for my dissonance amid these low tonguing hills,
this sprawl of open silences   vacant thoughts, passages paved over,
and i don't have anything kind to say about calgary, circa 1985, isn't that a
tragedy, because there are beautiful things there in that tragedy, and in the
interest of being resourceful i ought to mention them, since i owe my existence
to oil and gas, what does it mean to be honest in this extraction, does it mean:
          nausea   the same words, stanzas, figures roil, repeat, and sprawl.
the same strip mall, the same gas station, the same concrete hills, identical
monopoly bungalows breeding to the end of   the same used words,
same chain-stores, box-stores, the same automobiles shining in the immense
parking lots, the cookie-cutter children born to inherit the redundant
          vocabulary of vacuity   the same big sky, the paved   vacancies
between the constellations

alterity

the chronicles of itaguai relate that in remote times, at the auction of a circus that

had gone bankrupt in a region of south america that had never been visited by white

men, mercado viejo turned velvety with ash as even in the peaceful world of plants,

major aranda suffered the loss of a hand in a social revolution that took july's

motionless brambles, a couple of years ago don pedro damian shouted to his wife,

who was upstairs a few nights earlier, with one of the priests who were so richly

dressed that the men touched them to see if something strange was going to the sea

when the lookout blew his conch to announce that the fifty black ships came, as i

recall, at the end of september, to the brick floor of the cell a dutiful, orderly man

participating in the tumultuous finale with a pianist passed into a coma just beyond

the gray stone bridge my father dropped years ago, moonlit by the argentine central

siesta a wave moved ahead of the others, past the white gate in front of a newsstand,

a wave entertained the hope of finding the news vendor holding out the change for

the frogs riddled by el lampino's bullets in the depths of equatorial africa when the

stranger arrived, quite out of breath, at the metallic village where savage sewer

games shatter infinite fists in unending breath in deserted complaint uninhabited

for twenty years, arrived quite out of that montevideo afternoon on the outskirts of winds chasing one another, the french explorer, hunter and man of the world the

story of a great slaughter when i was a very small pygmy, when the first children

who saw the dark and slinky bulge approaching through the sea were still an old

couple next door hanging their "i don't know" and their "ideas" in the palms of

hands where someone crossed the night, dug his nails into a meteor and said:

years ago, between the peaceful world of plants
and the silence of an indifferent earth

fifty black ships swelled within me
and dreams of gold charged the horizon

quel avenir connaîtrais-je?
celui de mes frères et soeurs les esclaves?

i was then 4 years old, and saw my world
as vulnerable, as a far sail trembling under the gong

and saw, through volcanic courses
myself as a soldier facing the port of morning

my first act of ingratitude
arrived with the men on the coast

a procession of messengers
drums tuned to a different pitch

sharp, swift
and the vessels

drawn up at my feet
swollen with nothing

ribbed for hoarding
for loading, morning

molten between myself
and eternity

between gold, good, and bad
between the loss

or gain of lime
coffee, cashew

between the journey
que les anglais venaient de m'arracher

alors que le navire faisait voile
between soldiers and—

exhausted, having received
250 coups de fouet sur les jambes, les fesses et le dos

every morning
i became a soldier who could not be kind

every morning
i rejected my heart of hearts.

every morning
i blazed between my life and eternity

every morning
the impending departure of the ships swelled within me

every morning
i stamped my newly shod feet

bruggadung

i beat my heels into the grung

bruggadung

i planted my father's thunder

bruggadung

i received the earth's revolution

bruggadung

from the bottom rung

mon coeur se gonflait de fureur et de révolte

every morning

flowers flashed in the sun

le feu glorieux. le feu qui dévore et calcine

every morning

the british empire hungered and groaned within me

and a sense of despair, a life in my hands

a limp flesh clutched and wrung

a shadow dripped across an ocean

son ombre s'étendit sur moi comme un génie protecteur

a shadow dreaming of small stones

in my mother's abdomen, in the hands of a carib woman

small stones shot from *les fusils du blanc*

small stones swelling within the intrigue

small stones whose skins glistened

small stones pierced with arrows

small stones of raw commerce

small stones blinking at the first beam of dawn shot across the curve

of the burning earth, small stone eyes seeing the world as dew

small stones skidding through surf

small stones scattering into pelicans' wings

small stones spinning in afric, in arawak skulls

small stones percussing chance, small stones sparking in darkness

small stones of ackee seeds carried under the tongue

to flourish their future against babylon

small stones who marooned

small stones of mountains, *raisins de la colère*

small stone shuttles, drumstick tips

ne peuvent pas nous tuer elles glissent sur la peau

the captain's toy fleet *glisse sur la peau*

in the fine sea spray, in the gust of the town day

the years lead to the front door, past

de longues et lourdes siestes à l'ombre des manguiers

toward a brave morning on its way

. . . asylum seekers have come from Syria, Eritrea, Sudan, Yemen, Iraq and beyond. They arrive at Roxham Road after crossing thousands of kilometres by bus, plane and foot.

—*CBC News, February 26, 2017*

nameless to the news, welcome

amorphous file seeking asylum, stragglers in the sun's eye

vanguard of the welcome exodus, wandering toward

welcome in taxis, roxham border, the crossing

gravel path slimming through snow and spruce

disembarking and walking north rolling suitcases

behind, welcome plastic wheels shuddeirng, gravel cracking

children on hips, welcome toys and shoes stuffed

into shopping bags, family miscellany trundling

in this procession   crossing   this warped sphere

desire   a trail of welcome that scatters

back through darkness

exploding star liner

incandescence through which the equator

walks its tightrope back

Solidarity without Borders wants to mobilize the population to help migrants, and especially to send a collective message that they are welcome.
—*Montréal Gazette, August 6th, 2017*

welcome plaited black hair   welcome cocoa-brown faces

peering between sugar maple branches, welcome baseball caps and red ski jackets

clashing with the alternation of brown and green, welcome amid jack pine trunks

black spruce needles pointing toward one welcome or another, one state or

another, one constellation or another illuminating every direction at once,

everywhere welcome every place a possibility, welcome every thought a new

sojourn, truth elusive, every line branching and rebranching into every other

welcome, divining forward into hoarfrost, no indication of

eventual welcome rest or root a temporal confusion

is the future winter

across the border, or packed and shipped

back to the welcome

past, back to

. . . she had been living in Ft. Lauderdale since 2009 but left the United States last week because she feared being sent back to her home country.

—*Montréal Gazette, August 7th, 2017*

welcome   feared being sent so instead fled

in this news she is all of we, seeking, unsettled, unselved,

they is welcome she, turning inside theyself, turning theyself in—

      crossing into the arms of the buzz-cut border officer in southern québec

      arriving at the booted foot of the state, at the mercy. imagine,

      at the mercy of what another can imagine for they who have crossed

      a hemisphere, an imagination that has known only

      a backyard, a fence, a street, a town the size of a leaf

      must dream for them   welcome

. . . a two-day bus ride to the northern border where the family crossed into Canada, suitcases in hand.

—*CBC News, September 13, 2017*

welcome turning selves in, selves traveling through space, turning being in to paper

flesh become white fiber for deliberation, legality in question, self a question mark

welcome signatures, boxes checked on forms welcome dossiers deconstructed

sequences of numbers queued up to be filed, sorted, detained, catalogued, welcome,

interrogated, archived, speculated upon in the news, counted, and either welcome,

accepted, rejected, re-counted, queued up again, filed into a different queue, chased,

fled, welcome, or stalked in limbo in borgesian bureacratic labyrinths, trash-talked

by pundits, welcome, whispered about in polite living rooms, opined on from the

middle class on down, welcome, debated in wood-paneled parliament encircled by

welcome, by words, invoked to stoke fear, vilified as terror, as other, welcome, now

tossing on narrow army cots chrome and canvas reality, minimal without asethetic,

the furniture of state aid of newsflash

In the first six months of 2017, officials noted almost 4,500 illegal border crossings across Canada—3,350 such crossings were made in Québec.

—*CTV News, August 02, 2017*

welcome from ayiti after the earth liquefied

migratory aftershocks spread through new york

miami, houston, chattanooga for a decade welcome

working undocumented, and now montréal

living in flight, temporary as rent, as graffiti, as the turcot el

crumbling into st-henri, structural adjustment welcome

temporary and in flight welcome

to the entrance near the loading docks

the bleachers standing exposed to the wind your

collective living room, welcome the entire concrete east

end of montréal your barren yard

Between 100 and 450 cots have been set up in the Olympic Stadium. The asylum seekers will be housed in the area with concession stands just on the border of the actual arena. It's a windowless, concrete hallway.

—*CBC News, August 2nd, 2017*

welcome the generations carried in your heads

welcome the ghost cargo

essequibo

the unity of worlds

billions of slow forest eyes follow me, curved and pointed at their edges

the leaves blink, the slick leaves turn and read me as i pass, a glowing amber figure, an interloper with a strange culture of concrete and wires colonizing my gray matter, the dangling vines are letters my language can't decipher, the jungle floor is fallen leaves, decomposing maps, fermenting directions, lives steaming as they sink into the earth   is fired fronds in overlapping patterns above the sun-hammered black copper floor, veined glyphs that branch and re-branch into each other, is an inchoate language simmering down into the cosmic crucible, is leaves flattened and sinking into the earth's molten core without a whisper, is the echo of the canopy's nocturnal chatter, is an infinite archive of carbon-based letterforms, is a gibberish rustle in the underbrush, is the eyelid's crocodile skin, its reptilian braille thinking, is an imprint more ancient than paper, is decomposing into the bitter, gleaming sap of a literature, is a wink in the gloaming of homo sapiens, is an organic desire to continue without hubris, heaving and exhaling a fermenting mist that drifts up between the branches, that settles into moss in the grooves of rippled trunks, that sails up into the solid beams of light rotating down through breaks in the green, up into the insectile parliament in the canopy, and up again, the earth's exhale hangs above rot and ripening alike, the forest's   jaw groans

the dials of a half-million radios are tuned to the ocean, roaring white noise
in the conch of georgetown   jet engines launch our cellular clamor
        across the magnetic equator's clouded curve, fuselage streaks down
toward cheddi jagan international, suitcases straining in the cargo hold,
zippers aching to burst   foliage slithers out, t-shirts crinkle into
petals, pant-legs cinch into vines   shoes split into networks of roots,
roots identical to the brown rivers' jagged graphs that pierce the terrain
        books hang open   paginated, lolling fronds   denim seams
arise   green antennae receiving relatives' voices   cracking in through
the distortion of empire's metropoles   breaker   surf spiralling
ashore   the palms transmit and receive   voices of coromantee women
ringing out and feeding back   akan, twi, fante, bono, wasa, nzema, baule,
anyi   languages ground into silt word-fragments and flung by the
trade winds across the entire caribbean, their phonemes salted by the sea-
spray   sound cured by the air the ear, this entire country an ear facing
upward and listening, listening, receiving signals from the world, receiving
these weeping crystals of world-stories sprinkled over its narrative canal and
landing on its quivering drum

i too am nothing, *rien q'un pacquet d'eau sonore*   water darker than gold,
darker than what the liquid pupil can pierce, i too circulate in my charged
course, am rushing, am a sonic eddy in which human voices from everywhere
and every age at once   dissolve   standing on the bank of the
potaro, the verge of nihility   water and earth vibrating up through rubber
and marrow   brown river bending along its neural course, trees' light-
dappled leaves turning, conversing over either shore, spider foliage dangling
       an idea forming   hushed, knuckled roots clutching at soil
       roots come unfastened, plunging their digits into the sepia current
       a notion of home eroding where the water, where the body abrades the
bank   leaf-scales rippling along the potaro's surface, lumbar shape-shifter,
giant boa constrictor river moving under the blinking shadows, uncoiling into
a numinous clearing, light slowing to signal against shadow along its surface
       asemic coils unspelling over the rock drop

taut with awe, the falls' thunder bears down on being　　　liquid hammers
　　　　　we resonate, percussed numb　　　　mud-gold water
charges toward the slick rocks　　　the body's every locked　　　blue
atom strains　　　toward the current that is thoughts　　　we too are
water, we too are ire, brown, we too lean toward release　　　bones and
their tethering desires could liquefy and ease over　　　the teeth of the
continent open, and we stand in the infinite library of its
　　　　　rumination, pages decompose, histories compose into linked genetic
alphabets, mists form, white hanging in the air, a smoke that falls upward as
the water tumbles in its zigzag static　　　into whose charge mine would
dissolve, whose power exceeds, *moi qui n'est rien qu'un pacquet d'eau sonore*,
and as it rotates down toward the river's basin below, its helices carry the
reptile and the howler monkey, prism of the dew, blinking, reluctant leopard
of the slow eyes, marabunta poised to sting, extinction in slow electric strophes
cascading　　　into the smoking basin　　　into the yawning green

the force that drives the drone in our ears
            in its fixed jungle course   tugging at the roots, tearing at the soil
      pooling in our skin, pulling our sentences into babble, sucking at our
organs, our atoms   the arguments of cities in our ears
      parrot's green screech and awesome question mark of the scorpion
      frond's curve tonguing air, insects' hive and chatter buzzing over the roar
      the falls   rumble down down, all time ticks down
      columbus in the slow fall   entire amazonian races extinguished in a
foaming bead   flying upward   in a second finally released from the
clocks's gravitation   empires razed in the water's blink   and the tiny
golden frog, sharp as an arrowead   watches watches

NOTES

Much of this work was composed while listening to *Eternity* and *World Galaxy* by Alice Coltrane, and to early works by Barrington Levy and Gregory Isaacs.

Epigraphs: Derek Walcott, from the poem "Guyana" (1969), and from *Omeros* (1991).

Walter Rodney – Guyanese historian. He was also involved in politics, and formed the WPA (Working People's Alliance), in opposition to the PNC (People's National Congress) government of Forbes Burnham. Rodney was assassinated on June 13th, 1980, at the age of 38, when a bomb was planted in his car.

Mantra of no return – This section originated in, and quotes from, *A Map to the Door of No Return*, by Dionne Brand.

High School Fever – Passages in this section reference the deaths, at the hands of the police, of Neil Stonechild (November 25th, 1990), and Anthony Griffin (November 11th, 1987), as well as the Oka Crisis (July 11th – September 26th, 1990). Phrases have been drawn from articles in the *Globe and Mail*, *Montréal Gazette*, and the CBC web archives.

Bow – This poem, along with Essequibo, was a collaboration between myself, Laura Toma, and Kevin Yuen Kit Lo at LOKI Design. Both poems involved imposing passages from the book atop mapped images of the Bow and Essequibo rivers, then digitally abstracting the passages.

Zero Degrees – This section draws from *Seed Catalogue*, by Robert Kroetsch.

Alterity – Much of this section is composed of fragments from the opening sentences of stories in *The Eye of the Heart: An Anthology of Latin American Short Fiction*, ed. Barbara Howes.

Alterity – Other source-texts from which fragments have been abstracted and reassembled: *A Way in the World*, V.S. Naipaul; *Moi, Tituba, sorcière*, Maryse Condé; *Sun Poem*, Kamau Brathwaite.

These poems occasionally riff on phrases recalled from many years of reading Caribbean poetry. Countless poets have contributed a word, an idea, a translated line to this work, and to each I offer my enduring gratitude.

ACKNOWLEDGEMENTS

This book owes its existence to Dionne Brand, for support, editorial insight, and for showing the way.

This work is indebted to Tanya Evanson, whose close reading and detailed criticism proved indispensable.

These pages were eased toward publication by Kelly Joseph, Five Seventeen, Rachel Cooper, Peter Norman, Jared Bland, and by the collaboration of McClelland & Stewart.

As a book emerges, its presence must be announced, and this book was generously spoken for by M. NourbeSe Philip.

This work was completed at the Bundanon Trust Artist Residency in Australia.

*

Some of the works in this collection have appeared in *Jacket 2* and in *Carte Blanche*. The visual poem "Bow" was nominated for the *Carte Blanche* 3Macs literary prize, 2018.

Sections from this work have been performed at the Obey Convention (Halifax, 2016), and at the Word Travels Festival (Sydney, Australia, 2018).

A segment of this work was scored for musical performance by Jason Sharp. The composition, titled *Turning Centre*, featured Cheryl Duvall (prepared piano), Ilana Waniuk (violin), Jason Sharp (modular synthesizer, electronic processing), and Kaie Kellough (voice). *Turning Centre* was presented at the Music Gallery (Toronto, 2018).